COMMON GROUNDS

An Entrepreneurial Guide to the Coffee Shop Office

ANCIL LEA, III
AND FRIENDS

Common Grounds: An Entrepreneurial Guide to the Coffee Shop Office
by Ancil Lea, III and Friends

Cover Design: Darren Huckey

Visit My Blog and Sign up for Updates:
www.goancil.com

Follow Me!
Twitter: @ancilleaco
Instagram: ancil3
https://www.facebook.com/ancillea

COMMON
GROUNDS

An Entrepreneurial Guide
to the
Coffee Shop Office

ANCIL LEA, III
AND FRIENDS

Contents

Foreword

A ncil Lea and I have known each other for a long time. To many, Ancil is well-known by the multiple roles he fulfills – friend, family man, devoted disciple, businessman, soccer coach, and medical software guru, among others. Regardless of the multiple titles or roles with which Ancil is identified, there is one overarching characteristic that he lives out daily across all of his many personas and that characteristic is his innate ability to build and maintain strong relationships. I suspect that's at least one of the reasons Ancil identifies so well with the modern Coffee Shop.

You see, coffee is a great "connector." Some of the most lasting friendships were formed and some of the best discussions have been held over a cup of coffee. I would even say that many a business deal were consummated over a steaming hot cup of coffee. That brings me to the matter at hand – *Common Grounds: An Entrepreneurial Guide to the Coffee Shop Office.*

In this book, Ancil and his team have compiled stories, thoughts and other musings on life as it exists in the local coffee shop office. From the perspectives of the college student and young professional, to the solo practitioner and seasoned business executive, to the coffee shop barista, *Common Grounds* has it all.

Now that you have your copy of Common Grounds in hand, go find your favorite hangout. Order a fresh hot "cuppa Joe," say "hi" to all of your friends and colleagues and then settle in. While you read, be sure to take time to look around. Watch what's going on around you. See if Ancil's stories become your stories. I bet they will. In doing so, you'll probably find that you, Ancil and his team are all on common ground.

Have fun,

Dr. Jeff D. Standridge
The Innovator's Field Guide
www.JeffStandridge.com

Introduction

I f you are an entrepreneur or someone with the freedom to choose where you work, you might work from home like I once did. But have you ever considered using your local coffee shop as your office?

In 1991, I left the corporate world to start my own firm for consulting in and selling medical software technology. These were the days before the Internet and even cell phones, so I had to work from home to get my business started. That worked fine for a while, but I soon became lonely and discouraged trying to make it happen all by myself. I realized I needed to be around other people; loneliness wasn't good for my productivity or creativity. Maybe you feel the same way.

This is where the neighborhood coffee shop comes in. Coffee continues to be a central theme of my life and work. The evolution of coffee shops like Starbucks and Panera—and local shops like my home base, Blue Sail Coffee—has created an endless wealth of great coffee. But these coffee shops are so much more than the coffee they sell.

Coffee shops provide an environment that is conducive to my approach to life and business. There you can sit, have a conversation, and get to know more about someone—their needs, goals, and de-sires/dreams. Working out of a coffee shop allows for the personal interaction that a lot of us so desperately need.

Not only that, but conducting your business out of a coffee shop removes barriers and allows your clients to lower their defenses and be who they are. For me, when someone wants me to meet with them in their office, I feel uncomfortable. I'm on their turf, if you will. When we meet in a coffee shop, however, we're both on a level playing field—on common ground.

That's the idea behind Common Grounds. This book is a compilation of insight and personal encounters that I and other contributing authors have had while working at our local coffee shops. I believe that our stories and experiences will inspire and encourage you to adopt the coffee shop office.

So go on. Head on over to your local coffee shop, order your favorite drink, and discover the many benefits that the coffee shop office has to offer.

Enjoy!

Common Grounds

.

It Don't Come Easy

ANCIL LEA

"Only those who will risk going too far can possibly find out how far one can go". – T.S. Elliot

When we see a successful business we rarely truly understand what it took to get it there – the blood, sweat, and tears to make it all happen. There's a story behind each success.

Being an entrepreneur is not for the faint of heart. Most people don't realize what it takes to be successful. The costs to follow your dream or vision are incredible. The risks and sacrifices of starting your own business are immense.

My friend, Kyle Tabor, is a successful entrepreneur and owner of a local coffee shop called Blue Sail Coffee. He shared with me his story and it made me realize what I, and other entrepreneurs, live most days and don't really think about. When Kyle was in college, all of his friends knew what they wanted to be or do upon graduation, but not him. He explored many ideas. Upon graduation, he took the path of most to work for a large corporation, taking a job with one of the world's largest software technology companies. As he said, "I worked there for 3 months and hated it. This wasn't me."

Kyle quit his job and used what money he'd saved and traveled to Italy. He was very interested in cycling and watched the Italian version of "Tour de France" to see what it took to be a professional cyclist. While in Italy he was amazed that there was a small coffee shop on every block. He caught the vision of something special happening there – there was not just coffee but 'community' in these shops.

He came back home and started his first shop with a little money and a big vision. He poured everything he had into his new venture, sleeping on a small cot in the supply room at night. He was the only employee when he first opened. Now Kyle owns three coffee shops and has numerous employees. I so appreciate his vision, his work ethic and what he's accomplished!

For me, the coffee shop has been a place where I can share in community while chasing my plan or dreams.

Trying to get a new idea or company off the ground with little or no capital takes creativity, grit, and some degree of naiveté. It's hard to get going under these conditions. One of the main ingredients, however, is never being afraid of failure.

Since I have been in my career, my motto has been, "It don't come easy," from the title of a Ringo Starr song (written by George Harrison). It's not easy starting your own business! J. K. Rowling said, "Anything is possible if you've got enough nerve." However, to make it easier on your journey, you need others around you to provide a sense of community for energy, encouragement, and challenge.

So, a coffee shop is a perfect place for guy like me who had no money, but had the determination to turn my dreams into reality. And I'm thankful for other entrepreneurs like Kyle who are willing to share their story and encourage others to take risks and go for it.

Impromptu Meetings

ANCIL LEA

I pulled into a new Starbucks that was just put up close to my house without thinking much about it, other than being in need of a good, hot, rich cup of coffee on my way to meet up with my wife. After placing my order for a wonderful, tall, dark Italian roast, I stepped over to the side to add some cream in my coffee before jetting off down the road.

I hadn't noticed when I walked in, but sitting at one of the tables was an acquaintance of mine. He is an entrepreneur, business owner, consultant, and all-around guru. I had just thought about him yesterday and knew I needed to run something by him for his opinion. What an opportunity! At least for me anyway. He had his headphones on, so I walked up to him and tapped him on the shoulder. I said, "Hey man, how are you?" His response was perfect: "I've done a YouTube video, a webinar, and several calls from this spot this morning." And then he jokingly added, "Kind of a coffee shop office ... someone should write a book." Great minds think alike.

At that point, I asked if I could have a few minutes of his time to run something past him. He said yes and set his headphones down and turned to listen and engage. What I got from that 10-minute conversation could greatly impact my financial picture. I greatly value his thoughts and input. He has been successful for multiple companies, and does quite well. He was kind enough to take time with me.

This scene plays out so many times each day in coffee shops around the country, and probably around the world for that matter. These coffee shops, whether its's a Starbucks a local brand like my Blue Sail, have people working hard to make things happen for their business, their employer, or themselves. It's incredible who frequents these coffee shops.

I've seen millionaires, bank presidents, college professors, sales reps, college students, you-name-it, using these shops to get their work done, and most will stop to exchange conversation with you. Funny, in this electronic world of texting and messaging—in an impersonal world—coffee shops provide a place of coming together for business, friendships, ideas, romances, conflict resolution, etc.

Call it serendipity when you run across these moments in the coffee shop. Meetings that could change your financial picture or redirect your life to find your path could happen with someone sitting close to you. Find a person and start by asking how they are, and then go from there. May your path be blessed!

Net Neutrality

ANCIL LEA

R ecently, I was at a Healthcare IT conference in Little Rock, Arkansas. My friend, the executive director, of the Arkansas HIMSS chapter, made his way over when he saw me. He had just read one of my latest blog posts about the coffee shop office. He broadcast throughout the hall where we were, "You know, the largest deal I ever closed was in a Starbucks!" I truly appreciated his confirmation of the point I was trying to drive home in my blog post.

A coffee shop is the perfect "neutral ground" for a meeting. Something about having a hot drink in our hands, in addition to the overall relaxed atmosphere, makes it easier for us to drop our guard and be who we are, and maybe even a kinder version of ourselves.

Many of the deals I've closed and the strategic relationships I've formed have been over a cup of coffee. We both arrive and stand on even-footing; no one has an advantage or the upper hand. The playing field is level.

Over the many years of my career, one truism keeps coming back around again and again. People do business with people they like. Cultivating relationships and friendship is done over time. Spending time with someone and getting to know them is the best way to foster a long-term personal and business relationship—a bridge built that you both can cross for many years to come.

From the hipster to the baby boomer and beyond, we all find that the coffee shop holds something special for cultivating great relationships and advancing thought.

Funny thing, when I want to have a heart to heart with one of my kids, we'll go get a cup of coffee and talk. We both share a life update, discuss a serious matter, and/or a light-hearted laugh about what is going on in our lives. The cup of coffee is disarming and uniting; it brings people together to find some much needed common ground. And man, we could really use more of that in today's world.

The Drive

ANCIL LEA

Doing work from different places gives you different vantage points. Whether you're in a cubicle in a large corporation, state government, or an office with a door shutting out the rest of the world, each place gives you a different perspective on what work you're doing. They also give you access to resources, the ability to be a team, and more.

One of the things I've noticed over my many years of working out of a coffee shop is how well people work. As someone that values productivity, I'm constantly (though unintentionally) observing the work behavior of people throughout the course of the day. Many people in the coffee shop—whether they're a barista hustling to fill an order, a salesperson working on proposals or following up on leads, or a college student writing a paper—are diligent and focused on what they have to do to be successful.

Let me take a moment to express my appreciation to the millennials. I have recommended several of them to companies that come to me for hiring recommendations. I know they have been slammed as of late, but the ones I see are hard-working, encouraging, and loving individuals. And I've been around plenty of folks that aren't.

So, here's my shout-out to this group. They inspire and motivate me. Thank you for being who you are—don't stop!

Fuel for Creativity

KASSANDRA KLAY

A s an entrepreneurial woman, I choose to work in an office space that Fortune 500 professionals might envy. It's a space where creativity flows and overhead is a steal. It's my local coffee shop.

Holding meetings at a local coffee shop provides many creative advantages. For one, it provides neutrality. A coffee shop meeting puts all parties on a level playing field and provides a more relaxed atmosphere. Working in a more relaxed atmosphere allows individuals to stay focused on their agenda while allowing themselves the opportunity to think clearly.

Not only is it relaxed, it's positive. I've never walked into a coffee shop and experienced a negative atmosphere. Maybe it's because people are fueled with their favorite coffee, or maybe the ambiance of a coffee shop puts everyone in a good mood.

Being surrounded by fellow entrepreneurs seems to get the creative juices flowing. I never have a problem brainstorming ideas when I am in a coffee shop. The wheels in my head spin and the ideas flow freely from my brain. I manage to always get a lot of work done. I usually stop mid-brainstorming session because I must leave, which is a disappointment at times because the ideas are rolling out of my brain at a ferocious pace. Once that momentum stops, it's not easy to get it back.

Also, most entrepreneurs put in long hours, and coffee is a staple in their diet. During long meetings, a much-needed coffee boost can revive and energize a person when they are run down or exhausted. The coffee shop provides an eclectic menu of delicious coffees prepared by skilled baristas and barristers. When I am at home or in my office, I have the basic black coffee, so going to a local coffee shop and enjoying an iced latte is always a treat.

Another benefit of the coffee shop office is that a lot of entrepreneurs need a break from the traditional office or home office space. Many creative minds need a change of place, and a coffee shop provides that. Working constantly from the same office day in and out can get mundane and is not conducive to a creative environment.

Creativity is part of the fabric of entrepreneurship. And it's especially crucial to me as a romance author. I have friends that are authors too, and we enjoy getting together for writing sessions. A coffee shop not only feeds caffeine addiction, but also provides energy that fuels creativity and imagination. Many novels out on the market today have been developed and written in coffee shops all over the U.S.

Next time you are in a coffee shop, look around at the other people there. You will be surrounded by creative minds all working on a goal. Absorb that atmosphere and use that energy to work toward your next objective.

A Million Cups
and More
of Innovation

TODD JONES

"**H**ey, would you like to grab a cup of coffee?" How often have you heard that question at a networking event? Gathering around a cup of coffee with another entrepreneur is something that has been around for a long time.

Every Wednesday morning across the United States, companies share their stories with an audience of their peers. The event is called 1 Million Cups and is hosted by the Kauffman Foundation, an organization that helps drive entrepreneurship and innovation.

1 Million Cups started in April of 2012 in its hometown, Kansas City, Missouri, and has grown to over 100 communities. The centerpiece of each meeting is a cup of coffee. Members gather for free cups of coffee, meet other entrepreneurs, and listen to pitches from two different businesses. The group asks questions, gives feedback, and listens to the company owner tell what they need to help spread the word.

1 Million Cups events allow entrepreneurs, startup founders, in-

vestors, creatives, and other members of the business community to connect in a neutral location. The Kauffman Foundation realized that startup owners, though they socialized, were not intentional about helping each other share their work to connect with potential customers, investors, and team members.

These events meet in various types of buildings including innovation spaces, co-work spaces, colleges or universities, coffee shops, and other unique spaces such as a loft.

In a TEDx video, Kauffman team member Nate Olson said, "Communities are built over cups of coffee, over relationships. So we started with the hypothesis that if Kansas City's entrepreneurs could drink a million cups of coffee together, that we could fundamentally change the culture of entrepreneurship in Kansas City."

The word "innovation" is the idea of introducing something new, and, with the help of coffee, 1 Million Cups and the Kauffman Foundation are introducing new things to entrepreneurs every single week. Participants learn about new startups, new ways of doing things, new ideas, new connections, and the things that are innovating industries, such as digital marketing.

1 Million Cups is a fantastic way to formally introduce the idea of innovation over a cup of coffee with other entrepreneurs. The Kauffman Foundation offers a systemized way to start a chapter in your city. However, as entrepreneurs, we can use coffee to spur innovation in less formal ways. One business owner I know has set out to meet as many people as he can over a cup of coffee. As a result, he's made friends, connections, and even found business. We can do that as well.

Offer to have cups of coffee more often, listen to the stories of others, and build a relationship that matters.

Now, would you like to grab a cup of coffee?

.

Caffeinated Synergy

ANCIL LEA

B ack in the 90s, I had a medical software company that I started out of my house. Working from home is not all it's cracked up to be. The mystique is soon lost with children crying or needing attention, dogs barking, and the ultimate distraction or un-motivator of being alone.

The productivity killer in my life has by far been feeling alone. With no community around, it's easy to feel like I am not a part of anything. I may have the knowledge, contacts, and expertise to make a successful business, but I need to be around people. In the 2000s I started working from a small local coffee/breakfast shop and became fast friends with the regulars—artists, salespeople, professors, etc. who were also there working.

Fast-forward a few years, and the holy grail of coffee shops comes to town—Starbucks! Superb coffee, Wi-Fi, lots of people, and energy. I used Starbucks for many years as my home base. I used it to work from, making calls and having meetings with clients. It worked so, so well! I felt I was on to something. The staff was professionally trained to remember my name and what I wanted. It was my place. I would walk in with a client and the barista would call my name and know my order. I would meet and close thousands of dollars of business, and do my day-to-day work there.

The energy of being with others and feeling like you're a part of a team or community is so important to our success, mentally and financially.

The business lunch has been replaced with the business coffee. Being able to come together around a warm drink of java seems so desirable in today's world. It may have been all along and I'm just now discovering it. Business lunches have been historically critical to success and business development. I haven't tracked it over the years, but I would say the chances of gaining a client go up tremendously when you can sit down and meet face-to-face. The coffee meeting seems to be taking precedence these days. I think folks find it hard to go to lunch and spend an hour or two to talk business when they could spend a half hour doing so over coffee.

When we are a part of a community and are not alone, we are most productive in our work, whatever that may be. I think it's a truth for everyone across the board. Coffee shops provide that needed welcoming environment.

Brewing Goodwill

ANCIL LEA

Reality number one: the coffee shop is for your wellbeing.
Reality number two: you are for the coffee shop's wellbeing.

I f you're reading this today, chances are your traditional office setting has let you down in some way. Or worse, you have nowhere from which to base your work. In both instances, you need an option that provides for your needs consistently.

Using your local coffee shop as your office provides huge benefits, particularly in networking and availability, but using it well is not without commitment. Decide on the front end to be as enjoyable to the coffee shop as it is to you. Let's face it—no one loves the obnoxious coworker. Inside the walls or out on the patio of your local coffee shop is not the place for distracting people from their work, starting heated debates, or using what is offered without giving anything back.

Just because you're free from investing in rent and utilities doesn't mean you shouldn't invest and infuse goodwill into your new office setting. Consider these easy steps for brewing goodwill:

Step 1: Buy the coffee. (Or the scones, tea, smoothies, cakes—

whatever floats your boat, really.) Hopefully you're rolling your eyes alongside me at this no-brainer. The sad fact of the matter is too many coffee shop owners bewail the supposed customers who set up shop without investing in the business whose Wi-Fi they're currently utilizing—hence the push in recent years at giving out the Wi-Fi password only to paying customers. Without sales, your "office" closes. Take the money you used or the little you were saving for office rent and invest it where you are.

Step 2: Invite others in. You multiply your financial investment in the coffee shop when you invite others to join you there, whether for meetings with you or simply alongside you as another mobile worker. The more business you can help bring in, the more pleased owners and employees will be to welcome you in every day. You might even begin to get some routine perks!

Step 3: Learn names. I know, I know—another no-brainer. Both studies and personal experience speak volumes on the value of learning (and, of course, using) people's names. Names are the first part of everyone's story in life. Some may argue, but taking the mental effort to remember names demonstrates personal care in a way that little else does. Calling your local baristas by name solidifies a fact you need each of them to know you are invested in their work and in their lives. Making this clear opens up a relationship of possibilities. And finally...

Step 4: Ask good questions. Names are the starting point. Asking good questions both to baristas and to other customers allows you to begin utilizing the full value of the coffee shop network. Noticing when workers have been sick, who the regulars are, and what people talk about will allow you to step into the community around you. By no means does this mean you have to turn into a Chatty Kathy. Be free to focus. Accomplish tasks. Knock out to-do lists. Just be sure to take little steps of goodwill along the way. Your investment will reap dividends.

Remember, you have both the privilege and the power to bring about good for a place that seeks to secure good for you. Be responsible to that end.

Observations From A Barista

CHELSEY BECKER

Grind the coffee beans into the porta filter. Tamp the grounds. Lock it into the machine's group head. Count the seconds. Measure the ounces to make sure the shot pulls cleanly. Can you guess what I do? Yes, I'm a barista. I work at one of the many locally owned coffee shops that serves in-house roasted coffee and makes latte art in cute little mugs. It has a cool, hipster vibe with wood details, sleek graphic design, and local art hanging up on the walls. Little coffee shops like this one have been popping up all over the United States, and the type of people I see here might surprise you.

As a barista, I see a lot of different people every day. You might think I see only millennials, coffee connoisseurs, and aspiring artists, but those are only pieces of the diverse groups that come in. Yes, there are the college students who arrive to chug coffee while using the shop's Wi-Fi for writing papers. However, young parents, church groups, and, you guessed it, business professionals are also among my regulars.

While college students are a regular sight, the most common

thing I see from the espresso machine is a person sitting behind a laptop, holding meetings throughout the day. This person may be young or old, male or female, a seasoned pro or a newbie just getting started. What's most interesting is that they all support one another in different ways. They make connections, learn about each other's business, and give prospects to one another. When I first became a barista, this was not a sight I expected to see because, in my mind, a coffee shop was only a store like any other store. However, as time went on, I grew to understand that coffee shops, especially local ones, are so much more than that.

Coffee shops are micro-communities, full of different people who, when put together, make the perfect melting pot. No matter how versatile their walks of life are or how little they know one another before they walk in, the people within the community are there for one another. This might seem strange, but when you become a coffee shop regular and begin to see the same people every day, and the baristas learn your name and regular orders by heart, you start to feel at home. You realize that you've become a piece of something special. Who knew that a hot cup of coffee could warm hearts that much?

And in this coffee shop community, something magical happens to people that has been lost to many other social settings in this day and age: they get to know the strangers around them. I see this every day. The student sitting in the corner will run into a business-man at the condiment bar while grabbing a sugar packet, and they strike up a conversation. They introduce themselves before going on with their normal routines. A week later, they see each other at the shop and talk some more. Before you know it, that student has an internship. This happens more often than you would think. So many opportunities are made at coffee shops. I have made many connections myself simply working as a barista. I have received business cards, commissions for work, and support for my goals.

In fact, that is how I ended up writing this page.

Caffeinated Concentration

BROOKE BALLARD

Working on my certification studies out of a remote coffee shop has been a much different experience than working out of my office cubicle on-site. The coffee shop allows me to have flexibility to my studies and the pace at which I work. I am able to flavor my studying to my own style.

Having the relaxation of completing a certification at my own pace not only has increased learning experience but also outcome. It has also taught me self-management, which is critical not only to building a resume, but also to holding yourself accountable to complete a task. During the countless afternoons and evenings I've spent in local coffee shops dedicated to my certification studies, I have obtained 30-plus Sales and Technical Certifications around my area of focus—including industry-leading Microsoft Certifications, Intel, HPE, Cisco, and many more to grow my portfolio of knowledge.

The digital world we live in today, intertwined with the IoT (Internet of Things), has changed not only the way we work, but also the way we communicate. Working out of a coffee shop has given me opportunities to meet many people and continue the practice of communication. The best way to excel at any job is to be able to effectively speak about your role, solution, and company. The digital age has transformed the way we communicate to text, e-mail, skype conversations, and OneDrive/DropBox streamlined communication. Our world is losing sight of the importance of face-to-face communication. While mobility has enhanced the world we live in today, it has also stunted our ability to effectively communicate in person.

Immediately after graduating from college in Central Arkansas as a Women's Soccer Player, I moved to Gotland, Sweden, a small island outside of Stockholm. There I played soccer prior to beginning my technology career with HPE and, now, Insight.

During my time in Europe, I had to learn to communicate in different ways than ever before. I would bike with my laptop to a local coffee shop and spend hours in virtual classes to better understand the language. While the class helped me exceptionally, the biggest driver to learning the language was the opportunity to work out of the coffee shop. The locals from all over the island would come to do the same. Since our island in Sweden was very small, most people worked remotely for a corporation out of Stockholm. I had the opportunity to create business connections and friendships. I felt very little pressure and could communicate with those around me and complete the online courses at my own pace. I would not have had a similar experience being in a classroom or even a workplace office. I also found I was able to overcome the diverse language barrier much faster working out of a coffee shop with locals than in a classroom setting with others in a similar situation. Putting yourself in the track with others, specifically in a relaxed environment like a coffee shop, helps you to succeed.

Roasted,
But Not Toasted

DARREN HUCKEY

In 2005, my life changed significantly. Just a few years previously, I had started a creative agency and had two designers, a web developer, and an office manager working for me in a downtown office. We were producing some great work, but I had not entered into this business prepared. I just wasn't equipped to manage employees, payroll, and all of the things that go along with being an employer. The day-to-day expenses were piling up and I was losing traction every day. My ship was sinking fast, and I had to find a way out.

In order to rectify the situation, I had to make the difficult decision to close the office, lay off my employees, and revert back to a solo career working from home as I had done the five years prior to starting the agency. This was a very painful time in my life, but it allowed me to learn some very valuable life lessons that I am still applying today.

To ease the transition, I bought my first laptop so I could be portable. Since I didn't have an office any more, I knew I would need to meet with a client in public at times, and a laptop would be useful in those situations. As it turns out, getting a laptop was one of the best business decisions I ever made. It wasn't just a hip thing to do, but was something very practical. And as I soon found out, it enabled me the freedom I needed to handle the complications that immediately followed.

When I made the transition to work back at home, I instantly had a problem. I lived in a rural area at that time and had no options for high-speed Internet at my house. I was assured that providers would be headed my way soon, but "soon" is an ambiguous term. I had no way of knowing when a service provider would be providing service in my area. Being a graphic designer and web developer, having a decent internet connection was critical to the success of my business. So I had to figure out a solution to keep me afloat until I could get high-speed access at my house. Enter the local coffee shop.

At that time, Wi-Fi was becoming widespread, but public access in the city nearest us was still a little sketchy. Fortunately, most of the coffee shops realized the importance of providing Internet access to their customers while they enjoyed their cappuccinos. And since they opened earlier than most other places that may have offered Internet access, they became an easy choice for me. (Starting my day early while the world was quiet and I could think without distractions has been a long-standing practice for me.) So, after saying goodbye to my office, I wound up in an unlikely spot during my normal working hours, sipping on one of my favorite beverages in the process.

At first I wasn't sure how the coffee shop thing would work out. But then I read an article about a hot new startup company called Delicious Monster (delicious-monster.com). Their story was inspiring. They were a team of software developers who, at that time, worked together out of Zoka Coffee Roaster & Tea Company in Seattle. In seven months they were able to crank out their still-popular software for OS X, Delicious Library. This single success story sold me on the idea that I could be taken seriously working as a designer or web developer alongside a barista.

My eight- to ten-hour days at the coffee shop stretched out for probably a year or more before I was able to enjoy a high-speed Internet connection from the comfort of my own home office. But, even after coming back home, I continued hanging out at my favorite spot in the mornings, rubbing shoulders and sipping on a cup with clients and co-workers for the next several years. It wasn't something I was willing to give up on easily, and I continue to use the local coffee shop whenever I need a change of environment or an injection of creativity.

Take Time
To Smell The Coffee

DARREN HUCKEY

One advantage of working in a public environment, such as a coffee shop, is that you never know who you will bump into or what kind of relationship will develop from it. They may become a client, a colleague, a consultant, or maybe even your best friend. During the year or so that I worked exclusively from the coffee shop, I was able to build new relationships on both a business and personal level, many of which still exist over a decade later.

One example of this potential is best illustrated by something that happened to me while I was entering my coffee shop office one morning. A few people were sitting at a table near the door. I waved politely and said good morning to them without really paying much attention, and they returned the gesture. After I ordered, sat down, and got comfortable, I happened to look over at them again. I hadn't even realized it, but one of the men was an acquaintance of mine from several years before. I felt bad for not stopping to say hello to him, so I walked over to the table to offer an apology.

I caught up with what he had been doing over the last few years, and I discovered that he was about to launch into a new venture and was in need of logo development, branding, a new website, and design for print media as well. As he was talking, he remembered that I probably could do everything he needed. Our conversation naturally turned to business without any coaxing on my part, and he asked if I would be willing to help him with this new project. I told him I would be happy to help and asked when we could sit down and discuss the details. We set up a meeting where I could meet his team and begin working together.

When the entire team met, we put our heads together and began working to accomplish all of the goals of our client. My friend's consultant was a man by the name of Ancil Lea. I had met Ancil previously, but we had never really gotten to know one another. By working together on this project, Ancil was able to see the quality of my work as well as my work ethic. Once I completed the project with this client, Ancil and I started working on more projects together. We grew to be fast friends and still are to this day. Little did I know that a casual encounter with an old acquaintance at a coffee shop would end up launching my career with the company I am working for over decade later, let alone provide me with a valuable friendship that I continue to cherish.

The bottom line is this. If you find yourself working from a coffee shop, don't overlook an opportunity to build organic relationship in your work environment. You never know what blessings may come from them and what synergistic relationships may be developed. You'll never get that from a cubicle.

Working With What You Have

ANCIL LEA

Sometimes what seems to be a weakness, ends up being a strength. When you're struggling to get your business started with no capital and don't have enough cash for an office—and we can't or don't want to work from home—most of us end up in a Starbucks or local coffee shop. Though at first a foreign place, after a few visits, you get settled in and it becomes a place of your own.

How can you go wrong working in a place that has great coffee, Wi-Fi, a place to sit, and free aromatherapy! Once you have these basics, however, there is a much deeper world around you that you must discover.

Many around you are in the same boat! So many of us are trying to make it in whatever area of focus we have. Whether you're a software sales person, a college student, an artist, a graphic design professional, a pastor, or anything in between, we're all trying to make it and need a place to work, visit, connect, and thrive. The coffee shop fits the bill.

In one of my visits at a local coffee shop, I introduced myself to a guy and we hit it off with a conversation. Turned out that he's a writer. He produces content for several blogs and writes for one of the leading business magazines in our state. After our conversation, he introduced me to the owner of the business magazine and online media. I had coffee with him and began to write for them, too. What a deal!

This connection came from the guy next to me in the coffee shop, doing the same thing I was doing—working! (I also want to say how kind he was to do that for me!) So don't be discouraged by your lack of funds to get some big, plush office. It's not worth it! Start working in coffee shops and look for ways to connect with those around you. You'll be surprised who may be sitting next to you.

Focus Blend

DARREN HUCKEY

Distractions. Yes, that's one of the objections a person may have when considering adopting the coffee shop office. We automatically assume that productivity will suffer in an environment, such as a coffee shop, that has the potential for distractions. After all, music will most likely be playing; the front door will open and close repeatedly from all of the foot traffic; the milk frother sounds like a jet engine trying to take off; and a familiar face could walk up to your table and strike up a conversation at any given moment. These are legitimate concerns. So if this is the case, why is the coffee shop office an attractive option, and how do so many people seem to get things done there? How are they able to maintain focus as they tap away at their laptops? It actually may be easier than you think.

If you normally work from home, you know distractions are there every day. The dishes need put away, the light bulb needs changed, the laundry needs folded, the dog needs walked, etc. The list goes on. A hundred things run through your head as you sit in your office trying to crank out that new blog post, and procrastination can set in quickly. Being out of the house and in a new environment with new people, however, can help you be more productive without the distractions you may normally have. Even if you work in an office, a change in environment once or twice a month can work wonders to get you out of a rut and relieve stress.

Other factors also come into play. From a psychological perspective, being in an environment with other people who are focused on productive tasks can enhance your own productivity.[1] In other words, concentration can be contagious. One study implies that creativity can be stimulated and enhanced by ambient noise like the kind you hear at a coffee shop.[2] And of course, you have the caffeine from all of those wonderful espresso-based beverages. Focus in a mug.

You also have the less obvious things like the fragrant smell of freshly ground coffee beans wafting through the air. A modern coffee shop will have ambient lighting, soft music, and aesthetic furniture and decor as well. In other words, you'll find yourself surrounded by the very thing you are looking for: creativity and imagination.

---

1   https://www.newscientist.com/article/2090717-do-you-get-your-best-work-done-in-coffee-shops-heres-why

2   http://www.jstor.org/stable/10.1086/665048

Health and the Coffee Shop

ANCIL LEA

We have those moments in our lives that seem to crystallize meaning and focus. On the topic of health, Zig Ziglar, one of my heroes, once said, "You don't pay the price for good health. You pay the price of poor health. You enjoy the benefits of good health."

I've spent the bulk of my 29-year career in the healthcare industry (hard to believe), and today it's an industry caught up in overwhelming change. The technology solutions and services my company offers are all great, but sometimes we miss what healthcare really is—care for health—until we're the ones seeking care.

Fall is the time of year for high school football playoff games. The air is crisp, and it's perfect jacket (or sometimes coat) weather, even here in the South. A few years back, I traveled to Hot Springs, Arkansas to watch my son, the running back for our high school football team, play in one of these cherished games.

As I was helping get the run-through tunnel ready on the sidelines, I realized I was going to pass out. I headed to the bleachers and called for my wife before collapsing, barely holding on to consciousness. Our team trainer and others rushed over to help treat me and told me to "hang on."

It happened that an ambulance had just pulled up and, before I knew it, they loaded me up for transport. I lay in the back of the ambulance as we—the team physician (who happened to be a cardiologist from our town), the paramedics, my wife, and I—rode to National Park Medical Center in Hot Springs. I realized things were out of my control and I would not get to see my son play in his special playoff game.

When I arrived at the hospital, they immediately did a heart catheterization because they thought I was having a heart attack. I was clear, but they didn't know what was going on until the next morning when I was diagnosed with severe pancreatitis, which my doctor thought might be fatal. I spent the next two weeks in the hospital and the next couple of years going through multiple surgeries to try to return to health. It has been a journey of recovery.

Experiencing our healthcare system firsthand gave me a HUGE appreciation for nurses, physicians, support staff, and technology. As I work with these guys now, I see things differently, and, if I didn't before, I appreciate what great care is available to us. I'm sure it goes without saying, but I've also learned to take better care of myself by exercising, watching my diet, and reducing stress as much as possible.

But the first thing I did, once I could, was head back to the coffee shop to get back to work. You see, just before this happened, I had quit my job to restart my company. Losing your health can definitely derail your good plans and dreams. I had to climb back into the "game" and re-engage, and working from my coffee shop was just the ticket. The coffee shop gave me warmth, encouragement, and others who cheered me on in this new chapter of my life. Speaking of life, I'm glad I got to keep mine for a little longer.

Coffee Shop Etiquette

DARREN HUCKEY

I magine this. While you and your friends try to find a place to sit in the crowded cafe, some guy with his laptop is sitting alone at a table for six. He's watching either YouTube or Netflix at full volume and laughing hysterically at intervals. And if he bought anything at all, he polished it off hours ago. Your lunch appointment is now ruined because of this guy's inconsideration to the people around him.

Though this scenario is exaggerated, I'm sure we all have had a similar encounter and can remember how it made us feel.

When you set up shop at your local café (i.e., coffee shop), you can easily fall into some pitfalls. The key to avoiding these pitfalls is an ancient principle referred to as The Golden Rule: Treat others how you want to be treated.

As a working professional, it's easy to forget that the establishment you're using to make your living is primarily the livelihood of the cafe proprietor. Therefore, you should use your coffee shop office with caution. The following suggestions will ensure you remain an asset and don't become a liability.

Ask. If it's your first time at a particular coffee shop, simply ask if it is all right for you to sit at a table and work for an extended period of time. You don't want to be a laptop hobo—a person who stays beyond the normal battery life of a laptop—without permission. Asking in advance alleviates any awkwardness or resentment that could creep up unexpectedly with the proprietors.

Support. Support the establishment. If you are going to be at the coffee shop for several hours, be sure to order periodically. This will help cover the cost of the space you are taking up. Also, be sure to tip when applicable. Tipping shows your appreciation for people who are continually refilling your drink and putting up with your constant presence.

Limit. Limit your reach. Don't take up too much space by sitting at a larger table than needed or having your things spread out all over the place. This also means keeping your laptop cord "on the leash" and not strung out to catch the unaware. Don't dominate the airwaves by being loud on phone calls, and make sure you bring your headphones if you want to listen to your tunes while you work. Lastly, be mindful of peak hours and make room for groups who might be coming in for breakfast or lunch while you're working.

Schmooz. Be social. Don't just sit in the corner with your headphones plugged in the whole time you're there. Talk to people from time to time and build relationships with the coffee shop workers. You may be surprised at how much these interactions will bless you, and how they will bless others as well.

Keeping the above factors in mind will ensure your success when establishing your coffee shop office. When we are mindful of those around us and how they are affected by our actions, we are more likely to be encouraged by others to succeed in our undertaking. Simply put, be respectful to the establishment and its employees and customers, and you will be able to enjoy a long term relationship with your favorite java joint and grow your business in the process. Let's drink to your success!

Room for Cream

ANCIL LEA

One of the benefits of working from any coffee shop actually came to me during a meeting with one of my clients—a CEO of a well-respected specialty clinic. We always meet at a certain coffee shop downtown. I showed up early, ready for our meeting, but my client stood me up! That's what I thought, anyway.

After about 15 or 20 minutes, I sent a text to my client to make sure I was at the right place. (I've been known to show up at the wrong place or time). I found out that, on the way back from dropping his kids off at school, he received an urgent call from one of his physicians that he had to deal with. I ended up going to his office, which was only a block or two away, to follow up. It ended up being a great meeting. At the close of the meeting, he apologized for "standing me up," which I totally understood. Then he said something that made me realize even more how great it is to work out of a coffee shop. He said, "You know ... that's my hiding place. When things get overwhelming, I slip out and hide there to get my focus and perspective back." What an awesome statement!

When the Starbucks and the Panera's started popping up, I think I originally went there for those little retreats myself—great coffee, great atmosphere, and a place to think. I know these guys have created this atmosphere on purpose, and it truly works. Sometimes you just need to get away with your favorite beverage, read, think, and recalibrate life.

My client went on to tell me that his mentor had the same habit. He said, "We would look around for him, and he'd be missing. He had gone to his 'hidey hole' (hiding place) to get away."

We need a place to think and refocus. In all my experience working from coffee shops, I am continually reminded of the freedom I have to sit back, take a deep breath, and relax. In today's ultra-fast paced world, we need a place to think and refocus. I love being outdoors and definitely utilize walks, runs, bike rides, etc. to help in this area too. But, sometimes, during our busy work day or evening, we need a place to wrap our hands around a warm cup of coffee, sit for a moment, and think deep thoughts, or just clear our minds. Coffee shops are the place to do that.

With everything going on in our lives, we need to allow ourselves "room for cream," as I like to say. We need to give ourselves some room to decompress from life's busy schedule and daily demands. Sometimes we need to wrap our hands around a warm cup of coffee and sit for a while to clear our minds.

If your work responsibilities are weighing you down, make room for yourself. Grab your go-to source of caffeine and just sit and sip.

Apertif

ANCIL LEA

As I think about being an entrepreneur over these past 25 or so years, there are many days of great joy, offset by days of just work - hard work - trying to make it happen. A good daily routine helps in making things even out. Helps me to focus on the tasks or activity I need to daily to succeed.

Many days I've wondered what I've gotten myself into when I left 'dependable' income years ago for this life. Days I wonder if this is a blessing or is it a curse.

This inner desire to create solutions, find and drive business is where I've been placed. This is my world.

Here's what I do know: If I can do it, anyone can! But, it does take a dream, a plan, a solution, a product you're creating, coupled with hard hard work, and grit. The 'never quit' attitude is a must. Staying power!

A couple weeks ago I got a request on LinkedIn to have a teleconference and reconnect with someone I knew 1. I agreed to the teleconference. So, this person give me a call, and it starts out something like, "I was looking online for people who've been in the business for a long time. There are not many of us left, then I saw 'ol

Ancil' is still in there plugging away and I just had to reach out and see how you're doing."

The years of change that have occurred in the healthcare industry coupled with the fantastic advancement in technology has made it a crazy ride. Throw in governmental regulation and the promotion of technology in the healthcare industry makes for a wild and crazy market, full of opportunity.

During my career, one trite saying has stuck with me – "The harder you work, the luckier you get". When you work hard good things happen. I spoke to a very successful entrepreneur the other day, and I asked him about business development. He told me, "When I want more business, I just work harder." Could it be that simple? Bottom line is that you can have what you want if want it bad enough, and put not only your mind, but yourself to work.

And where's the best place to do it – from a coffee shop!

Follow Me!

Twitter: @ancilleaco
Instagram: ancil3
https://www.facebook.com/ancillea

Visit My Blog and Sign up for Updates
www.goancil.com

A Word of Thanks

To my team that helped to get this book across the finish line and has put up with all my crazy ideas and direction! You're help means so so much to me!

Team:
Darren Huckey
Kim McPherson
Laura Wiles
Suska Jones
Makenzie Evans
Amy Cantrell
Todd E. Jones
Rebecca Wilber

Writing contributors:
Darren Huckey
Kassandra Klay
Brooke Ballard
Todd E. Jones

Special thanks:
Kassandra Klay

Awesome book layout and design:
Darren Huckey

Photography by:
Makenzie Evans
Stormie Perry

Also:
Thanks to my family for enduring all the questions from people about this book and not having a clue what it's about and what to say. Thanks for believing in me and my dreams. I love you and couldn't make it without you!
Mr. Blue Sky
Dad